Introduct
to the M

A Guided Tour

MacOS 13 Ventura Edition

© 2023 iTandCoffee

All rights reserved. No part of this book shall be reproduced, stored in a retrieval system, or transmitted by any means, electronic, mechanical, photocopying, recording, or otherwise without written permission from iTandCoffee. No patent liability is assumed with respect to the use of the information contained herein. Although every precaution has been taken in the preparation of this book, the author assumes no responsibility for any errors or omissions. Nor is any liability assumed for damages resulting from the use of the information contained herein.

Special Sales and Supply Queries

For any information about buying this title in bulk quantities, or for supply of this title for educational or fund-raising purposes, contact iTandCoffee on **1300 885 420** or email **enquiry@itandcoffee.com.au**.

iTandCoffee classes and private appointments

For queries about classes and private appointments with iTandCoffee, call **1300 885 420** or email **enquiry@itandcoffee.com.au**.

iTandCoffee operates in and around Camberwell, Victoria in Australia.

iTandCoffee
Relax, we'll help you get iT

Introducing iTandCoffee ...

iTandCoffee is a Melbourne-based business that was founded in 2012, by IT professional Lynette Coulston.

Lynette and the staff at iTandCoffee have a passion for helping others - especially women of all ages - to enter and navigate the new, and often daunting, world of technology and to utilise technology to make life easier, not harder!

At iTandCoffee, **patience is our virtue.**

You'll find a welcoming smile, a relaxed cup of tea or coffee, and a genuine enthusiasm for helping you to gain the confidence to use and enjoy your technology.

With personalised appointments and small, friendly classes – either remotely, in our bright, comfortable, cafe-style space or at your own place - we offer a brand of technology support and education that is so hard to find.

At iTandCoffee, you won't find young 'techies' who speak in a foreign language and move at a pace that leaves you floundering and 'bamboozled'!

Our focus is on helping you to use your technology in a way that enhances your personal and/or professional life – to feel more informed, organised, connected and entertained!

Call on iTandCoffee for help with all sorts of technology – Apple, Windows, Android, iCloud, Evernote, OneDrive, Office 365, Dropbox, all sorts of other Apps, getting you set up on the internet, setting up a printer, and so much more.

iTandCoffee
Relax, we'll help you get iT

Introducing iTandCoffee ...

If you are in small business, iTandCoffee has can help in so many ways – with amazing affordable solutions for your business information needs and marketing.

Here are just some of the topics covered in our regular classes, books and videos:

- Microsoft Office Products and Microsoft 365 – OneDrive, Word, Excel, PowerPoint
- Introduction to the iPad and iPhone
- A Guided Tour of the Apple Watch
- Bring your Busy Life under Control using your technology.
- Getting to know your Mac and The Photos app on the Mac
- Understanding and using iCloud
- Taking and Managing photos on the iPhone and iPad
- Managing Photos on a Windows computer
- Windows basics
- Travel with your iPad, iPhone and other technology.
- Keeping kids safe on the iPad, iPhone and iPod Touch.
- Staying Safe Online
- Making the most of your personal technology in your business

The iTandCoffee website (itandcoffee.com.au) offers a wide variety of resources for those brave enough to venture online to learn more: handy hints for iPad, iPhone and Mac; videos and slideshows of iTandCoffee classes; guides on a range of topics; a blog covering all sorts of topical events.

We also produce a regular Handy Hint newsletter full of information that is of interest to our clients and subscribers.

Hopefully, that gives you a bit of a picture of iTandCoffee and what we are about. Please don't hesitate to contact iTandCoffee to discuss our services or to make a booking.

We hope you enjoy this guide and find its contents informative and useful. Please feel free to offer feedback at feedback@itandcoffee.com.au.

Regards,

Lynette Coulston (iTandCoffee Founder)

Introduction to the Mac
A Guided Tour
TABLE OF CONTENTS

WHAT ARE YOU RUNNING ON YOUR MAC?	5
New in macOS Ventura	6
YOUR MAC AND ITS 'USER ACCOUNTS'	7
LET'S START WITH THE MENU	9
New look for 'About this Mac' (macOS Ventura)	9
WHAT ARE YOUR PREFERENCES?	10
Preferences becomes Settings under macOS Ventura	10
TURNING YOUR MAC ON AND OFF	11
Powering On your Mac	11
Turning your Mac Off – Normal Shut Down	11
Turning Off your Mac – Forced Shutdown	11
Putting your Mac to Sleep manually	12
And then there is the 'Log Out' option	12
SLEEP AND PASSWORD SETTINGS	13
New Lock Screen System Settings (macOS Ventura)	13
And make sure your Mac requires a Password to unlock	13
Does your Mac log in without a password? (Changed in macOS Ventura)	14
Unlocking your Mac with Touch ID	14
New Touch ID & Password System Settings in macOS Ventura	15
DOES YOUR MAC ALLOW YOU TO 'RIGHT-CLICK'?	16
LET'S TALK GESTURES – SCROLLING, SWIPING & MORE	17
How to scroll up and down using the Trackpad	17
Scrolling using Magic Mouse	18
LET'S TALK ABOUT FILES AND FOLDERS	19
THE DESKTOP	21
A quick way to change the Wallpaper	22
Quickly Tidy a Messy Desktop	23
THE DOCK	24
What is The Dock	24
Controlling those Black Dots	24
Quickly Quit App from Dock	24

Introduction to the Mac
A Guided Tour
TABLE OF CONTENTS (cont.)

Controlling what Apps stay in Dock when not running	24
New Location for Dock Settings (macOS Ventura)	25
New in Ventura – Easy App Removal from Dock	26
MENUS AND THE MENU BAR	**27**
Application Menus	27
Status menus (Controls)	28
Customising the Menu Bar	28
Introducing the Control Centre	29
Configuring the Control Centre (changed in Ventura)	29
Using the Control Centre	31
Spotlight Search	31
Siri	32
Notification Centre	33
CONNECTING TO WI-FI	**35**
THE APP STORE ON YOUR MAC	**37**
Discovering the App Store	37
Different App Stores for Mac and iOS	37
Checking for App Updates	38
Automatic updates to your Apps	39
Getting Apps that are not in the App Store	39
MISSION CONTROL	**41**
Viewing all the windows that are open	41
If Mission Control is missing from the Dock	42
Setting up your Mission Control preferences	42
App Exposé	43
LAUNCHPAD	**44**
Launchpad is like the iPhone Home Screen	44
Put Apps into an App Group	45
Drag 'Favourite' apps from Launchpad to the Dock	45
Other ways of opening LaunchPad	45
Adding Launchpad back to the Dock	46

Introduction to the Mac
A Guided Tour
TABLE OF CONTENTS (cont.)

STAGE MANAGER	**47**
A new look for Desktop in macOS Ventura – Stage Manager	47
THE BIN (OR TRASH CAN)	**49**
SOME COMMON KEYBOARD SHORTCUTS	**50**
Managing Windows, Dock, Apps	50
Cut, Copy, Paste, Select, Undo	51
Sleep, log out, and shut down shortcuts	51
Document/typing shortcuts	52

What are you running on your Mac?

Apple regularly releases updates to the 'Operating System' that runs on our Macs. Apple's Mac operating system used to be called OS X. In 2016, OS X changed to macOS.

There is a major upgrade to the Apple Mac operating system released every 12 months, around October.

The different versions of the Mac operating system are given a number and a name. The current version is **macOS 13 Ventura** which was released October 2022.

The previous versions were, macOS Monterey (2021), macOS Big Sur 11 (2020) macOS Catalina 10.15 (2019), macOS Mojave 10.14 (2018), macOS High Sierra 10.13 (2017), macOS Sierra 10.12 (2016), then OS X 10.11 El Capitan (2015), OS X 10.10 Yosemite (2014), OS X 10.9 Mavericks (2013), OS X 10.8 Mountain Lion (2012), and OS X 10.7 Lion (2011), and OS X 10.6 Snow Leopard (2009). (We won't go back further than that!)

Since OS X 10.6 Snow Leopard (2009), it has been possible to easily upgrade your Mac to each year's new operating system using the Mac **App Store** – by downloading the free upgrade via the Internet, and then installing it.

OS X 10.7 Lion in 2011 brought **iCloud** into our world, which meant that it was no longer necessary to 'plug in' an iPhone or iPad to synchronise the data on these devices with that on the Mac. iCloud has allowed 'syncing' of data to happen magically! In fact, with its arrival, you no longer needed a computer at all to get content on to your Apple Mobile devices.

In this guide, we will be looking at screens, options, and instructions for using **macOS 13 Ventura**. For previous versions of the Mac Operating System, please refer to earlier edition books by iTandCoffee. Enquiries are welcome at enquiry@itandcoffee.com.au.

If you are using a version other than Ventura, you may see differences in the 'look' of the screens and the options/features that are provided and supported. While much has remained unchanged, significant changes have occurred in certain apps like System Preferences (now called **System Settings**).

We'll look shortly at how to determine what version of the Mac Operating System you are currently running.

What are you running on your Mac?

New in macOS Ventura

Throughout this document, we refer to various changes that have arrived with macOS Ventura – a large majority of which relate to changes to System Settings.

Below are specific sections that discuss some of the more significant changes (as well as the corresponding page number).

New look for 'About this Mac' (macOS Ventura)	9
Preferences becomes Settings under macOS Ventura	10
New Lock Screen System Settings (macOS Ventura)	13
Does your Mac log in without a password? (Changed in macOS Ventura)	14
New Touch ID & Password System Settings in macOS Ventura	15
New Location for Dock Settings (macOS Ventura)	25
New in Ventura – Easy App Removal from Dock	26
Configuring the Control Centre (changed in Ventura)	29
A new look for Desktop in macOS Ventura – Stage Manager	47

Your Mac and its 'User Accounts'

One of the things that is fundamental to any computer is the concept of 'User Accounts'.

Your Mac will have at least one User Account, and that user account will have a password associated with it (even if that password is 'blank' – which is not a great idea from a security perspective!).

If more than one person uses your Mac, your Mac can have multiple user accounts.

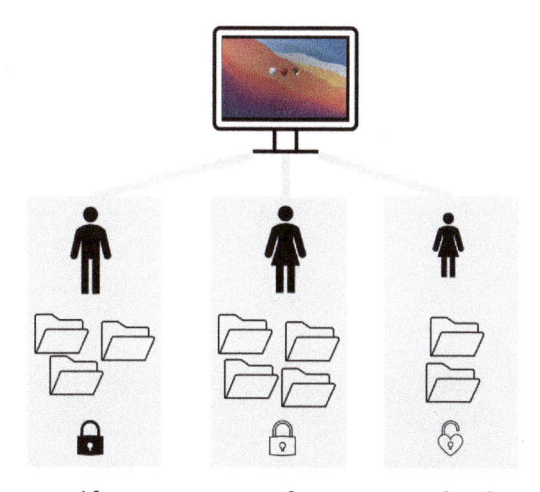

Each user account provides a separate and secure area for that person's data – a set of files and folders that are only visible to that person when they are signed in to that user account.

Each person's user account can be also signed in to their own iCloud account - which means they can see the same data from their Mac user account as what they see on their iPad and iPhone.

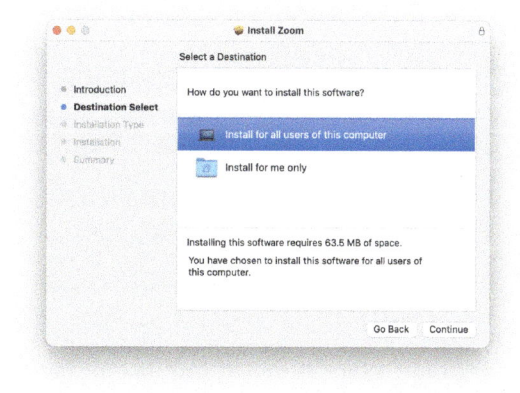

Anyone signed in to a different user account on the Mac will not see files and folders from other users (unless those users specifically choose to share certain folders, which is unusual).

The apps on the computer can generally be used by all users (unless, during installation, an option is chosen to only provide the individual user with access). An example of an install process. is shown on the right.

Your Mac and its 'User Accounts'

There are two main types of user account – **Administrator** and **Standard**.

Your Mac will have at least one user of type **Administrator**.

Other users can also be set up as Administrators or as 'Standard' users. Children can be set up with additional parental controls, using something called 'Screen Time'.

An Administrator has superpowers that Standard users don't have. Only an Administrator can install new apps or update/upgrade the Mac.

Only Administrators (Admin users) can change certain areas of System Settings – for example, those relating to users of the Mac, security, privacy, and more.

For these critical actions, a screen will always pop up, asking for authentication. Here are a couple of examples of places where the Admin user must enter the password (or provide a fingerprint, if one has been set up) for that account to proceed. In cases where the account currently being used is not an Administrator account, the Username must be filled in as well – i.e. it will not be auto-filled.

I know that people who are new to technology or Mac will often think that they do not have a 'user account' or that they do not need a password for their Mac.

Quite often their Mac has been set up to automatically sign in without asking for a password, which means that this very important password is forgotten or never known – which can then create problems down the track, when changes are required.

My message to all readers of this set of guides is that it is crucial to know the Username and Password details for your Mac's Administrator account.

While this password may have been set up to be the same as your password for your Apple ID, it is generally an unrelated, different password.

We will look shortly at how you can ensure that this password is required every time your Mac is turned on, and after a short period of activity.

Let's start with the menu

The menu can be found by clicking the at the very top left of the screen.

This menu has various options that are important to the use of your Mac: options for turning the Mac on and off, sleeping, logging out and restarting. We'll talk about these a bit more shortly.

New look for 'About this Mac' (macOS Ventura)

The **About this Mac** option gives quick information about your Mac's type, year of purchase, physical configuration and current operating system. This screen has changed significantly with Ventura. Its Monterey equivalent is shown on right below.

The version of the Operating System you are currently running is shown towards the bottom.

The options that were previously along the top in the older About screen are now available in **System Setting**s, under the **General -> About** option. We will look at System Settings shortly.

The menu also hosts an option to access the Mac's **App Store** (which may also be an icon in your Dock).

The **Force Quit** option allows you to 'kill' an app that is misbehaving. We'll cover this **Force Quit** option a bit later.

What are your Preferences?

Preferences becomes Settings under macOS Ventura

Throughout this guide, there will be frequent references to various setup options for the Mac.

These system-wide settings are managed from the **System Settings** App, previously known as System Preferences. (For those familiar with Windows, this is like the **Control Panel**.)

System Settings on the Mac is the equivalent of (and now more like) the **Settings** app on an iPad and iPhone (for those who also have one of these devices). In fact, in macOS Ventura.

It can be accessed in a couple of different ways:
1. Click on the 'settings' icon shown in the line of apps at the bottom of the screen (called the Dock, which we will describe shortly).
2. Alternatively, you can get to **System Settings** from the Apple symbol at the top left of your screen. i.e. -> **System Settings**.

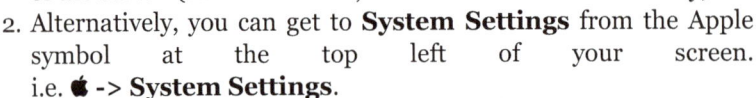

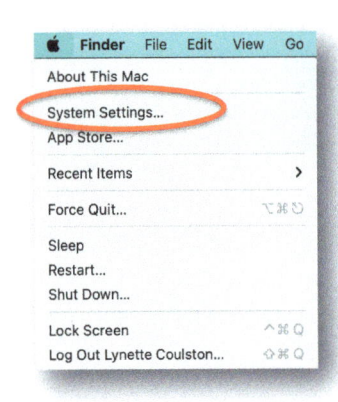

For those of you who previously used earlier versions of the Mac operating system, below right is the previous 'look' of System Preferences. As you can see, the new look is quite a change – and takes quite a bit of getting used to. Locating re-organised settings can be quite a challenge at first!

We will look at various System Settings throughout this set of guides.

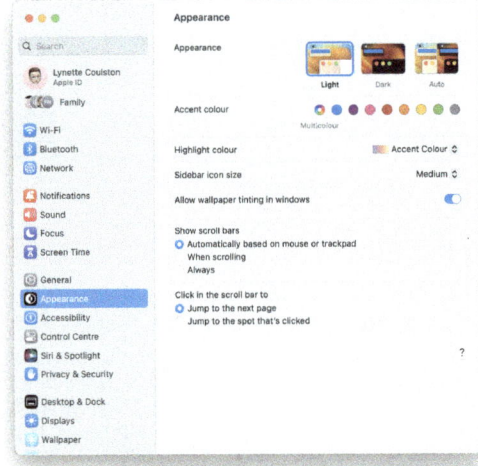

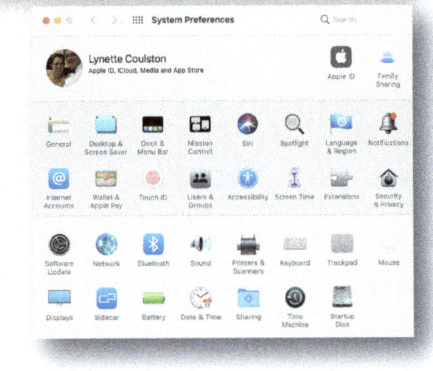

Turning your Mac on and off

The first thing a Mac owner needs to know is how to turn their computer **On** and **Off**, and to understand the concepts of putting a Mac to **Sleep** and to **Log Out**.

Powering On your Mac

Hopefully, you have already worked out this one.

On an iMac, the 'on' button is at the back of the screen, bottom left (when you are facing the front of the screen).

On the MacBook, the **On** button is at the top right of the keyboard.

Turning your Mac Off – Normal Shut Down

The method of turning off that should be used in the majority of cases is to select on the Apple Symbol at top left and select the option **Shut Down**.

If your mouse or trackpad is not functioning properly, but you still have a working keyboard, use the following combination of keyboard keys to shut down your Mac in a controlled way:

> **Control-Option-Command-Power** or
>
> **Control-Option-Command-Eject** (if you have a keyboard with an 'eject' key)

Turning Off your Mac – Forced Shutdown

Hopefully this won't happen too often, but if you do need to force your Mac to shut down – perhaps because it is stuck on the 'spinning beachball of death' and won't respond to anything you do – hold the power button down until you hear/see your Mac switch off.

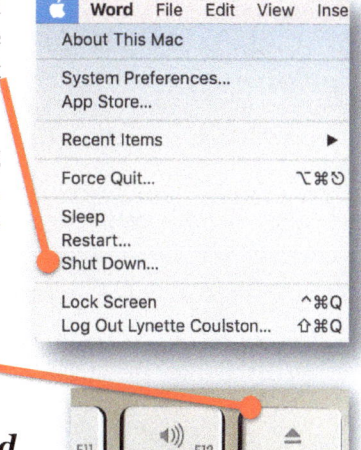

Don't do this unless you absolutely must – as it can occasionally leave something in an 'inconsistent' state and may cause problems. You will also lose any unsaved work.

Turning your Mac on and off

Putting your Mac to Sleep manually

It is not necessary to 'Shut Down' your Mac every time you have finished using it. You can quite often just put it into **Sleep** mode.

Sleep mode means your device is conserving energy but still able to 'wake' for certain events. It is like when your iPad or iPhone screen goes black (also a 'Sleep' mode), but it has not been turned off.

For a MacBook, just close the lid to put your Mac to sleep – or quickly press the power button.

On any Mac, put your Mac into Sleep mode by going to -> **Sleep**. Or use the following combination of keys (i.e. keyboard shortcut):

    Shift-Control-Power   or
    Shift-Control-Eject   (if you have a keyboard with 'Eject' key – see above).

And then there is the 'Log Out' option

Many people don't use the 'Log Out' option on their Mac.

It is really only relevant and used when the Mac has more than one 'user account'.

The **Log Out** option will close all active apps (warning first if you need to save any files) and return to the '**Log In**' screen (as shown below).

If you do have multiple user accounts set up on your Mac, make sure that each person 'logs out' of their account when they are finished. Leaving multiple accounts 'logged in' can dramatically slow down the Mac.

We won't go into this further here, as this guide is focused on 'getting started' – not on more advance setup topics like multiple user accounts.

Sleep and Password Settings

It is a good idea to set your Mac to go to sleep (i.e. turn the display off) if there is a period of inactivity, and to ensure that your Mac requires a password when it is 'woken up' (or turned on).

New Lock Screen System Settings (macOS Ventura)

These options used to be all under the Battery option in **System Preferences** in Monterey but are now found under the **Lock Screen** option in Ventura. (There are also some relevant settings in **Battery** and **Displays** option.)

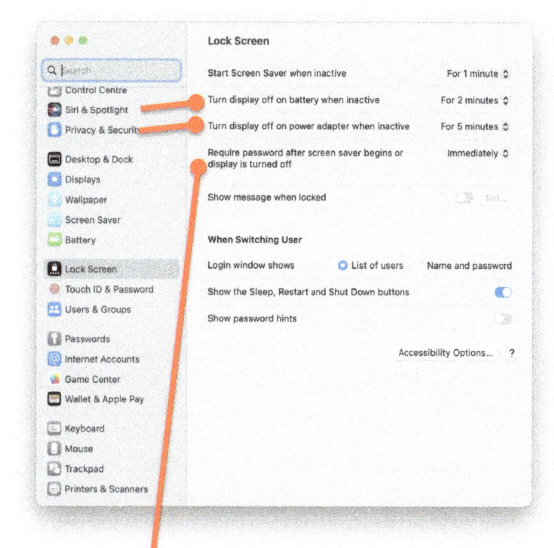

Click the **Turn display off when inactive** option (of which you there will be two for a MacBook, one for battery and one for power adaptor) to reflect the inactivity time after which the device should be put into sleep mode.

If you find your Mac is going to sleep too quickly, make this a bit longer – although not too long for the battery option, as this will drain the battery quickly.

And make sure your Mac requires a Password to unlock

From a security point of view, all Macs should have a passcode that is required to unlock the device after it is turned on or woken up.

As mentioned earlier, every Mac has an Administrator password that MUST be remembered for any updates to be applied to the Mac or for Apps to be installed.

If this password is not required on a regular basis, it can be very easy for this password to be forgotten.

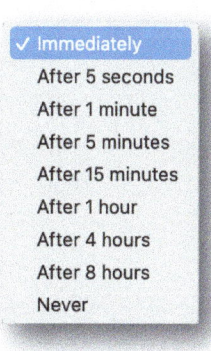

The Lock Screen option in System Settings has the **Require password after screen saver begins or display is turned off** setting, where you can define a period after which the password is always required. This can be **Immediately**, or can be, or a longer period – or Never (which is definitely not recommended).

Sleep and Password Settings

For any important **System Setting** like this one, you will need to provide authentication to complete the change, by providing the password that you use to sign in to your Mac when you turn it on.

This assumes that your current user account has a type of Administrator.

If your current account is not one with this type of access, you must enter the username and password for the Mac's Administrator account to be able to apply any change to this area.

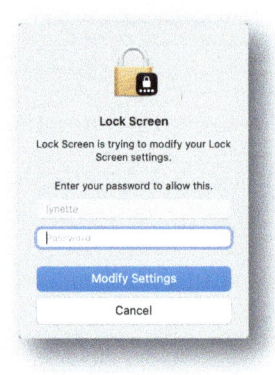

Does your Mac log in without a password? (Changed in macOS Ventura)

When you turn on your computer, do you find that it logs straight in without requiring a password?

This is because of a setting in **System Settings -> Users and Groups**.

If **Automatic Login** is showing 'On', change this to 'Off' to force the password's entry each time you turn it on.

You will again need to authenticate with your administrator account's password to complete this change.

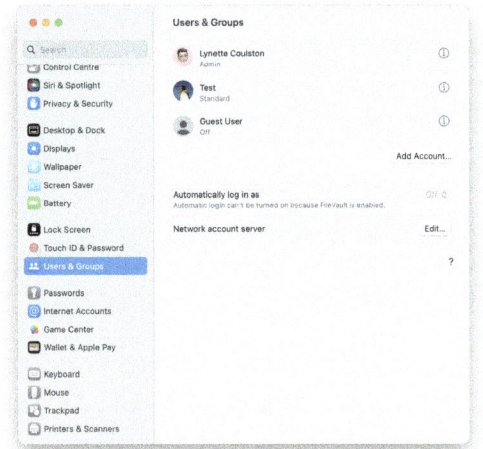

Unlocking your Mac with Touch ID

If you have a newer MacBook Air or MacBook Pro, you will have a handy alternative to entering your user account's password in most situations.

This feature is called Touch ID – where resting your finger on the button at the top right of your keyboard (above the **delete** key) can be used in place of entering the password.

(Note. The user account will still have a password – so you must not forget this, as the password is sometimes required in some places where Touch ID not an option.)

Sleep and Password Settings

New Touch ID & Password System Settings in macOS Ventura

To set up this alternative form of authentication, visit
System Settings -> Touch ID & Password

To get started, choose + **Add Fingerprint**. You will be required to enter your user account's password to proceed.

Follow the instructions to add your fingerprint. You can add up to 3 fingerprints.

Each fingerprint that you add can be given a name – just click on the name underneath each to enter your custom name.

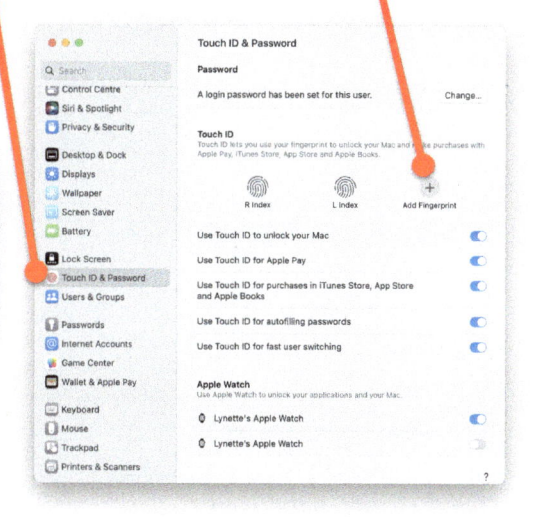

In the options below the fingerprints, choose the areas you wish to use Touch ID for authenticating.

Does your Mac allow you to 'right-click'?

Depending on the type of Mac you have, you may not have realized that you have a 'right-click' capability on the Mac. This feature is not enabled by default, so many people think it is not available on Mac.

If you are experienced with using a mouse, you will generally be well-versed in the use of the 'right-click' of the mouse to bring up the 'context sensitive menu' for the thing on which you have right-clicked.

On the right is the set of options I get when I 'right-click' on a file in Finder.

On the Mac, you can activate this 'context sensitive menu' using the keyboard shortcut, **Control-**☐

To enable the right-click – known as Secondary Click on your Mac – for the Mac's the mouse or trackpad, visit

- **System Settings -> Mouse** (if you have a mouse) or
- **System Settings -> Trackpad** (if you have a trackpad).

Select the **Point & Click** tab at top.

For the **Mouse**, the options to choose from for **Secondary Click** are Off (not recommended), **Click Right Side** and **Click Left Side**.

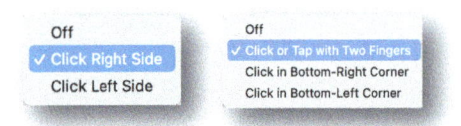

For **Trackpad**, the options to choose from for Secondary Click are **Off** (not recommended), **Click or tap with two fingers**, **Click in bottom right corner** or **Click in bottom left corner**.

It is important to remember that the 'right-click' function is also available by holding the Control key as you click the trackpad or left-click the mouse.

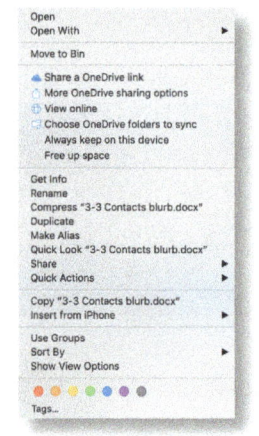

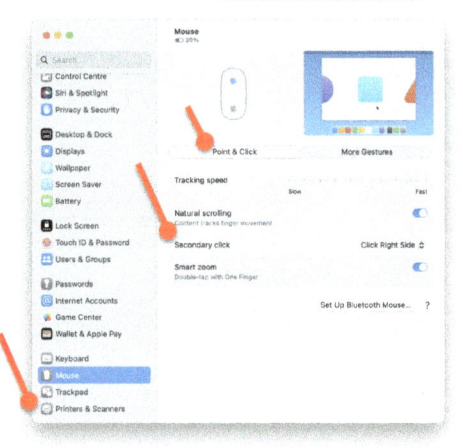

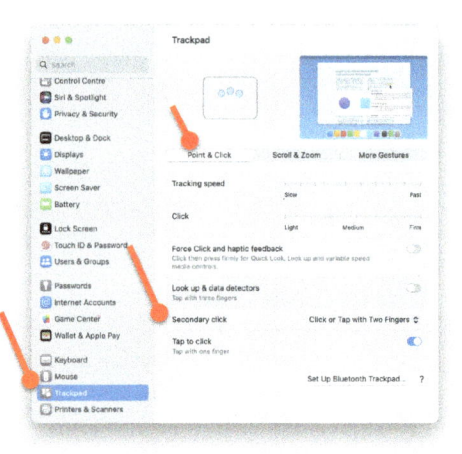

Let's talk Gestures – Scrolling, Swiping & more

We've already looked at a few gestures for your Trackpad and Mouse. It is well worthwhile to explore the various gestures that you can use on your Mouse and Trackpad, in the **Mouse** and **Trackpad** options of **System Settings**.

Hover your cursor over each option that is shown, and you are provided with a graphic at the top that shows you just what that option does and illustrates the gesture.

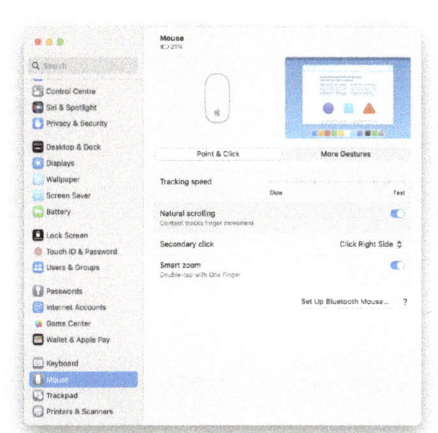

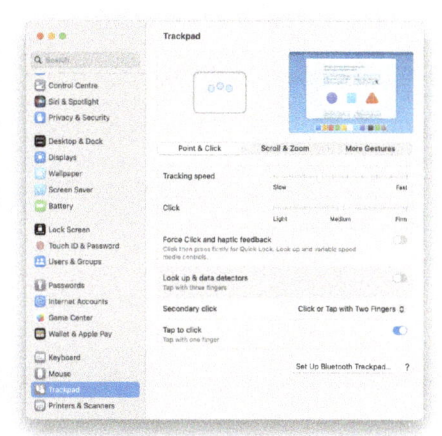

How to scroll up and down using the Trackpad

If you have a Trackpad, one very important gesture to know about is the 'scroll up and down' gesture.

Scrolling is achieved by **dragging two fingers up and down** on the trackpad.

The direction of scrolling is determined in **System Settings -> Trackpad**, in the **Scroll & Zoom** view.

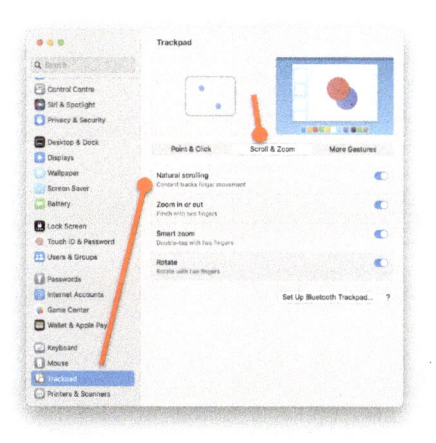

Turn on **Natural Scrolling** if you prefer the screen contents to move in the same direction as your finger movement.

Turn this off if you prefer the opposite.

Let's talk Gestures – Scrolling, Swiping & more

Scrolling using Magic Mouse

To scroll using your Apple Magic Mouse, just drag your finger up and down the surface of the Mouse

As for the Trackpad, the default scrolling direction is **Natural scrolling**, under the **Point and Click** view of the **Mouse** option of **System Settings**.

If you prefer the screen to move in the opposite direction to your finger movement, turn off **Natural scrolling**

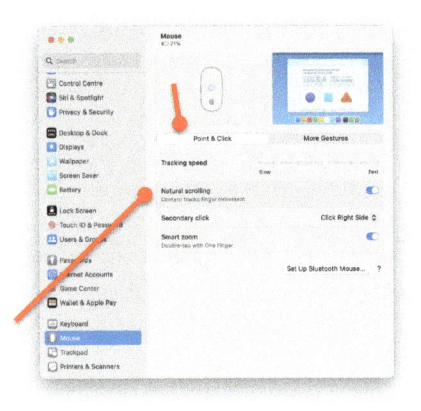

Let's talk about Files and Folders

An important concept to understand before we get into more detail about the Mac (or any other computer) is the concept of 'Files' and 'Folders'.

Everything on a computer is a file or a collection of files. Apps are files (or collections of files); a photo is a file; a document is a file; a spreadsheet is a file.

Folders are collections of files (and perhaps other folders), providing a way of organizing your files – effectively, your file cabinet on your computer.

Let's consider a real-life analogy. Think about a room with a set of filing cabinets.

The 'room' is a folder. Within the 'room' folder are 'filing cabinet' folders.

Within each filing cabinet are several 'drawer' folders. Within each 'drawer' folder is a set of 'suspension file' folders. Within each of these are 'manila folder' folders. The manila folders hold the pieces of paper – which are the files.

Each file has an 'extension' that determines the type of file that it is - **.jpg**, **.docx**, **.xlsx**, **.pdf** and many more. Applications on the Mac have the **.app** extension. (Note. If you don't see 'extensions' for your files, this is because of a Finder Preference – which we'll cover in our second guide in this series.)

Sometimes, something that looks like a file is really a folder containing lots more files. An example of this is your **Photos** library in a folder called **Pictures**, and any .app file.

Let's talk about Files and Folders

Finder is the app on your Mac that manages your files, folders, applications, etc. **Finder** is always on when your computer is running.

To display a Finder window, click the Finder icon in the Dock – which is always the bottom left icon in the Dock.

As mentioned, in Finder, it is possible to create folders and sub-folders in which to store your files.

There are various standard areas in which your files and folders can be stored – Documents, Desktop, Downloads, Pictures, Movies, Music are some of the main 'areas' provided by Apple.

Finder allows for the viewing of files and folders in different ways, sorting of folder contents, searching for files and folders, and so much more.

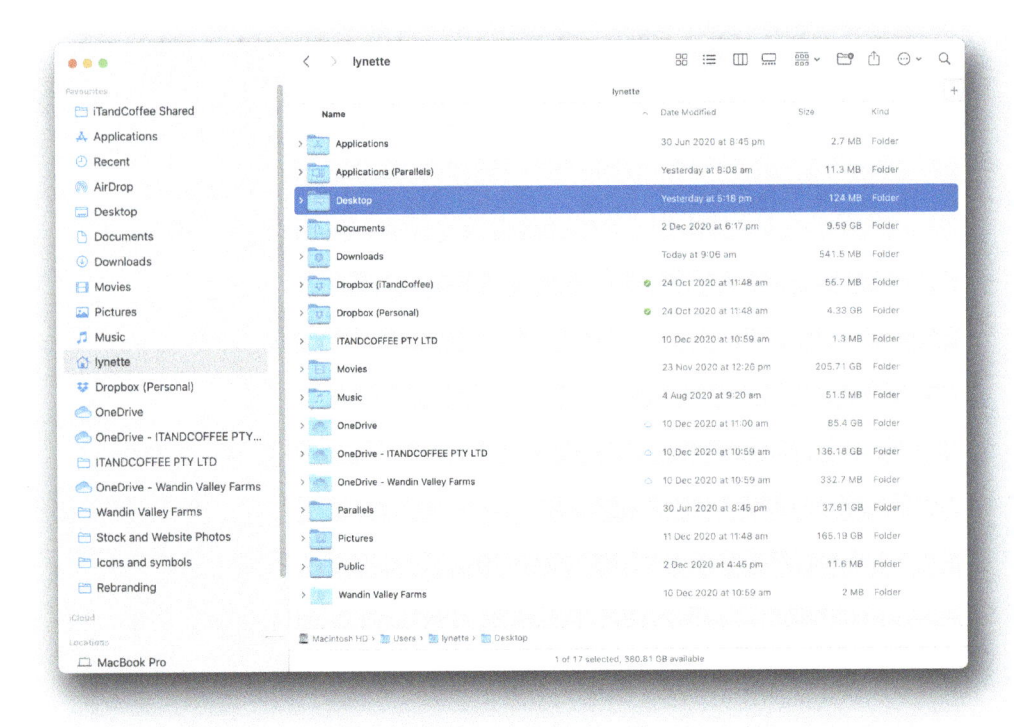

We'll cover lots more about Finder in the second guide in this series (called "Files, Folders and Finder").

The Desktop

The **Desktop** is the background area of your screen. But that's not all it is.

It is just like any other area on your computer for storing your files and folders. As such, it can always be viewed, and its files and folders managed, in your **Finder** app.

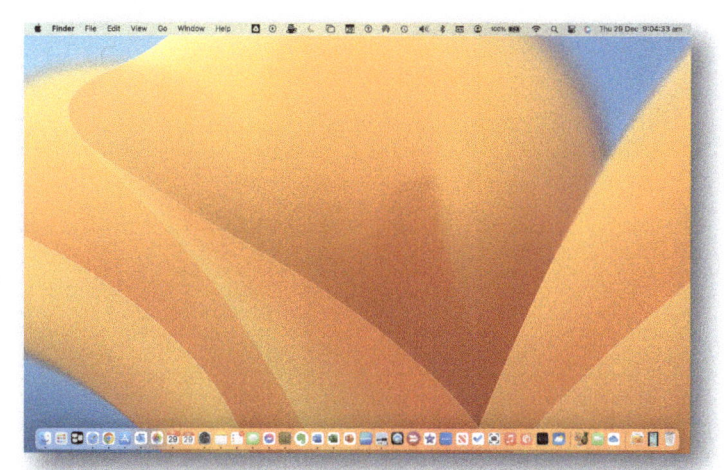

The main difference with the Desktop storage area (as compared with other storage areas on the Mac) is that any files/folders stored in this area are displayed as icons on the main background screen.

Storing files and folders on your desktop can provide quick access to frequently used items.

However, it is a good idea to try to keep the number of files and folders on your Desktop to a minimum, as storing too much on your desktop can slow down your computer's start-up and operation.

The Desktop may display icons for hard disks, CDs, and any servers connected to your computer – this depends on the 'Settings' that have been established for the Finder app.

The background of the Desktop may display an image from Apple, usually indicating what version of the Mac Operating system (macOS) you are currently running. In the example above, the Desktop image shows one of the standard **Ventura** images.

Alternatively, the background screen image can be a chosen personal photo. In the **Photos** App, bring up the required photo and choose the Share symbol, then **Set Desktop Picture**.

The Desktop

The preferences for your Mac's Desktop image (and more) can be managed from the **System Settings** App.

Click on this icon in the dock (the line of apps at the bottom of the screen, which we will describe shortly) to open your **System Settings**.

Alternatively, you can get to **System Settings** from the Apple symbol at the top left of your screen.

To choose the background for your Desktop – from either a set of standard Apple-provided images or your own photos - visit the **Wallpaper** option.

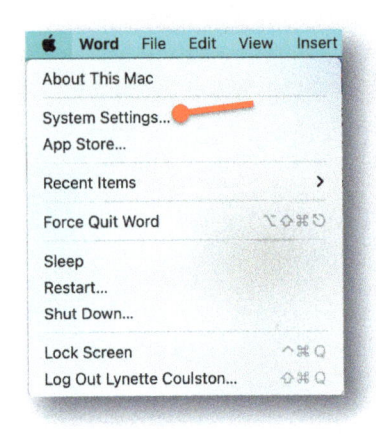

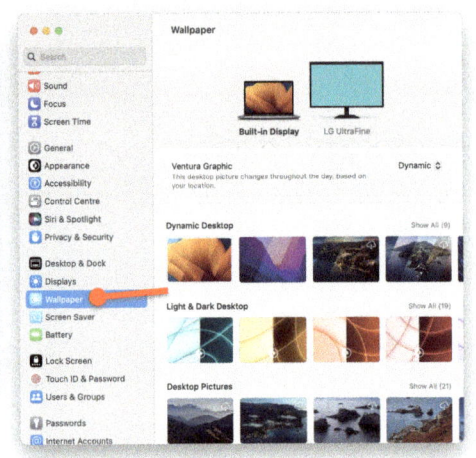

You will see various options for your desktop Wallpaper (background). Try them out, to see which one you like!

A quick way to change the Wallpaper

Right-click (i.e. secondary click) on any vacant space on the Desktop to see the set of options shown on the right.

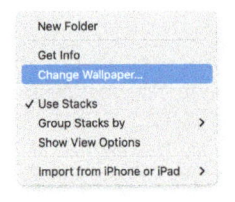

Change Wallpaper gives you a quick way of jumping to the **Wallpaper** option of **System Settings** (as described above), to choose a new Wallpaper.

The Desktop

Quickly Tidy a Messy Desktop

As mentioned earlier, a messy, cluttered desktop may have a performance impact on your Mac.

macOS Ventura provides an easy way of cleaning up your untidy Desktop. In fact, this feature was introduced several years ago by macOS Mojave.

Simply right-click in a vacant space on the Desktop and choose **Use Stacks**

Your screen will magically arrange its content by type of file, with a 'stack' icon representing a set of many files.

Click on that icon to view the contents of the Stack. The stack icon will be replaced with a 'down-arrow' icon.

To collapse the Stack again, click this down-arrow icon (example shown on right).

We'll cover more about this feature in the fourth guide in this series, **All Sorts of Handy Tips.**

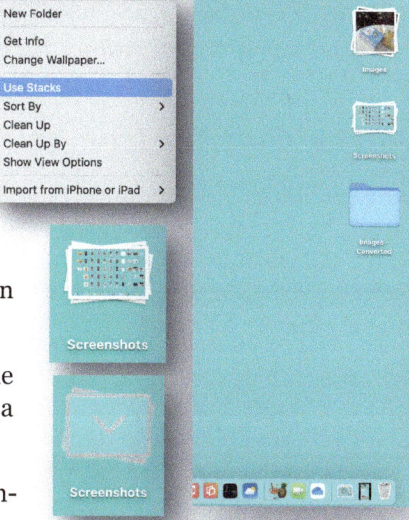

23

The Dock

What is The Dock

The Dock – usually showing along the bottom of your Mac's screen - is intended to show the Apps that you use most frequently. Just one click on an app in the Dock will open it. (There is no need to 'double-click'.)

By default, the Dock appears across the bottom, but you have control over where it appears. It can appear at the left or right side as well (and we'll look at where to change this shortly).

Controlling those Black Dots

It is important to note that, **whenever an app is currently running**, it will appear in the Dock and it will have **a black dot** underneath it – see the above image (and image on right) for an example of my own Dock, where several apps are currently running.

Another thing that is important to note is that, even if you close all the windows of an App (and we'll talk more about apps and app Windows in part 3 of this series of guides), the App itself may still be running and showing a black dot. It needs to be Quit to fully close it – something that can be done quickly using the app icon in the Dock.

Quickly Quit App from Dock

For each item in the Dock, it is possible to access a 'shortcut menu' that provides several options for that Dock item. To access this menu, 'right-click' on the item in the dock (or Command-click, or two-finger click on trackpad, if that is what you have chosen for your MacBook).

For any app that is currently running and that you don't need to be using right now, choose the **Quit** option to close the app.

Controlling what Apps stay in Dock when not running

You may find that certain apps 'disappear' from the Dock when they are Quit, and others stay.

Whether the app stays in the Dock when it is not running is up to you.

The Dock

The shortcut menu available when a Dock item is right clicked includes an **Options** sub-menu, which has a set of options that will differ according to whether the app has been previously set to 'Keep in Dock' or not:

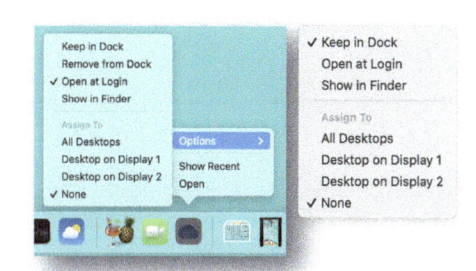

- **Remove from Dock** to remove an app that showing in the Dock when not currently running. It can be re-added later from the **Launchpad** (covered soon).

- **Keep in Dock** will have a tick when an app that is running has been already 'told' to stay in the Dock. If it is not ticked, click on this option to choose to keep the app in the Dock when it is not running.

The Dock can also show the 'recently used' apps in a section towards the right (as indicated above), with vertical lines to delineate this section of the Dock. Only apps that have not already been marked as 'Keep in Dock' will appear in this area.

This section of the Dock can be turned off in your **System Settings** - we cover this shortly.

Any apps that show in this Recents section can be dragged across into the main section of apps, which does the same thing as ticking the 'Keep in Dock' Option.

New Location for Dock Settings (macOS Ventura)

Customisations to the Dock are managed in > **System Settings** > **Desktop & Dock**

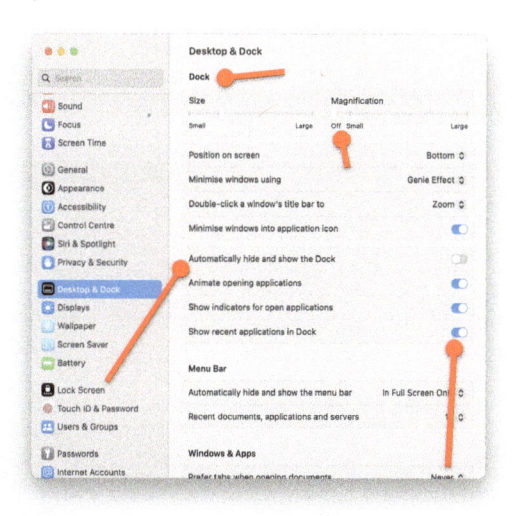

The top section, headed **Dock**, provides various options for changing the appearance and characteristics of the Dock.

Change the **Magnification** of Dock icons (this is what makes the apps 'grow' when you hover the mouse over them), the **Size** of dock itself (which impacts the size of the icons), the **Position** of the

The Dock

Dock (bottom, left or right), whether it is always visible, whether it appears/disappears, and more.

I recommended keeping the **Magnification** set to fairly small (or off), as it can be annoying to see your Dock icons grow huge when you hover over them.

If you are frustrated that your Dock keeps disappearing, untick the **Automatically hide and show the Dock** option.

And, if you don't want to see the section of 'recently used' apps in the Dock, turn off the **Show recent applications in Dock** setting.

New in Ventura – Easy App Removal from Dock

Ventura has provided an even easier way to remove an app from the Dock.

Simply drag it out and, when the word **Remove** appears, let go.

If the app is still running, it will stay in the Dock until it is Quit, when it will disappear from the Dock.

This is the equivalent of 'un-ticking' the **Keep in Dock** setting

Menus and the Menu Bar

The Menu Bar at the top of the screen is normally always visible – unless the App you are using currently is in 'full screen mode'. (We'll cover this in the third guide in this series – **Backups, Apps and Preferences**.) If the Menu Bar it is not visible, there is also a new option that may be causing this. We'll cover this shortly.

On the left side, this bar contains the **Apple menu** and **Application menus**.

The right side shows **Status menus (aka Controls)**, **Spotlight Search**, **Siri**, and **Time (and Notification Centre)**.

Application Menus

The **Application menus** on the left-hand side of the menu bar change to reflect **the App that is currently active**.

To make a running App the active App, simply click on a window for that app (or open it if not already open).

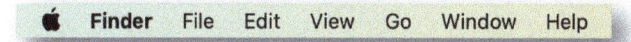

For example, the image above shows that Finder is the active app, and the menus shown relate to the Finder App.

Typically, the App menus include **File, Edit, View, Window**, and **Help** menus. Other menus specific to the active app will also appear here.

Here is the set for my Safari app.

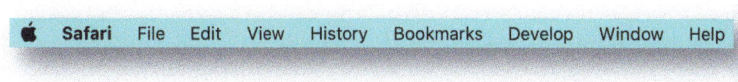

Just click on a menu to see the drop-down list of their options. On the right is the set of options available for my Safari's **File** menu.

For most apps, this is where you will find the **Print** option.

27

Menus and the Menu Bar

Status menus (Controls)

Status menus display information about, and provide shortcuts to, System Settings and app settings – for example, Wi-Fi status, battery level indicator, current time. These are also known as 'Controls'.

In the example below, you will see icons for several of the third-party (i.e. non-Apple) apps that I have on my Mac – including OneDrive, Google Drive, Fantastical, and Owly.

Clicking on any of these options will provide some options and/or information for that app or System Setting.

For example, clicking on the battery icon will show some information about the battery.

If the icon relates to a System Setting (which the battery icon does), you will find that the bottom option in the list gives you quick access to the System Setting screen for that setting. In the example shown here, **Battery Settings** takes you straight to the System Settings associated with Battery.

Customising the Menu Bar

macOS Big Sur brought significant changes to the Mac Menu Bar in 2020 – with a different look for the icons, and a different way of managing which icons/controls appear in the Menu Bar.

Big Sur also brought the **Control Centre** to Mac – similar to that which we see on the iPad and iPhone (and we'll look at this in more detail shortly).

To manage whether the Menu Bar is visible at all the times – or whether it disappears automatically when you are working within an app – go to **System Settings -> Desktop & Dock** (same option as we saw earlier for the Dock), to the **Automatically hide and show the menu bar** option. I usually choose to only hide the menu bar when in full screen mode.

Menus and the Menu Bar

In a significant change under macOS Ventura, the preferences that control what icons you see in the Menu Bar have moved to a new **System Setting** called **Control Centre**.

Introducing the Control Centre

The **Control Centre** icon in the Menu Bar was introduced in Big Sur in 2020.

The idea of the Control Centre was to provide a place where you can find a range of key Controls for your Mac – things like Wi-Fi, Sound, Do Not Disturb, Airdrop, Display brightness, Battery, etc – without having to include all these Controls as icons in the Menu Bar (if you don't wish to see them there).

For controls that appear in the Control Centre, you will have to option to choose whether to ALSO show that control separately in the Menu Bar.

Note that certain controls will not show in the Control Centre – Clock, Spotlight, Siri and Time Machine. But you can still decide whether you want these **Controls** to show on the Menu Bar

Configuring the Control Centre (changed in Ventura)

The configuration of the Menu Bar's **Control Centre** and the Controls (icons) that appear in the Menu Bar is, under Ventura, controlled from the new option **System Settings -> Control Centre**.

This option has three main sections headed **Control Centre Modules**, **Other Modules** and **Menu Bar Only**.

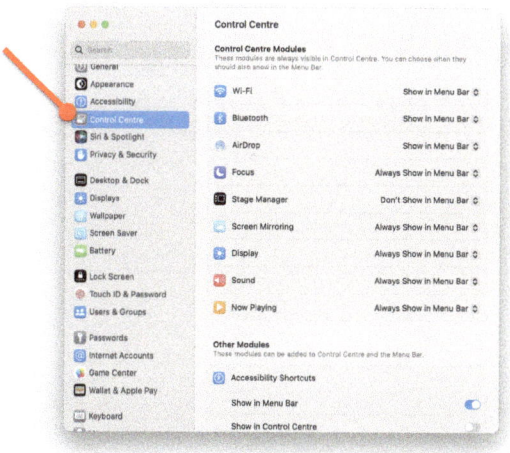

29

Menus and the Menu Bar

Control Centre Modules section shows the settings for the 'always visible' Controls.

These controls will always be shown in the Control Centre, but you can choose if you also want them to appear in the Menu Bar.

Other Modules section shows those controls that you can optionally choose to show in the Control Centre and/or Menu Bar.

You will see that for the **Battery** 'module', you also have the option to **Show Percentage** for that Control.

Menu Bar Only section (see bottom image on right) shows the Controls that are only shown in the Menu Bar and not in the Control Centre, allowing you to choose to not show them in the Menu Bar if desired.

The exception to this is the Clock control, which must always appear at the right end of the Menu Bar.

Choose **Clock Options** to choose the format of your Mac's clock – to show the date (or not), to include the day (or not), and various other option (see image below).

I must say that I do love having the date always showing at top right of my Mac's screen. I refer to it so often!

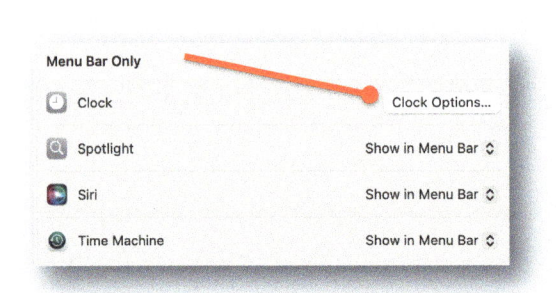

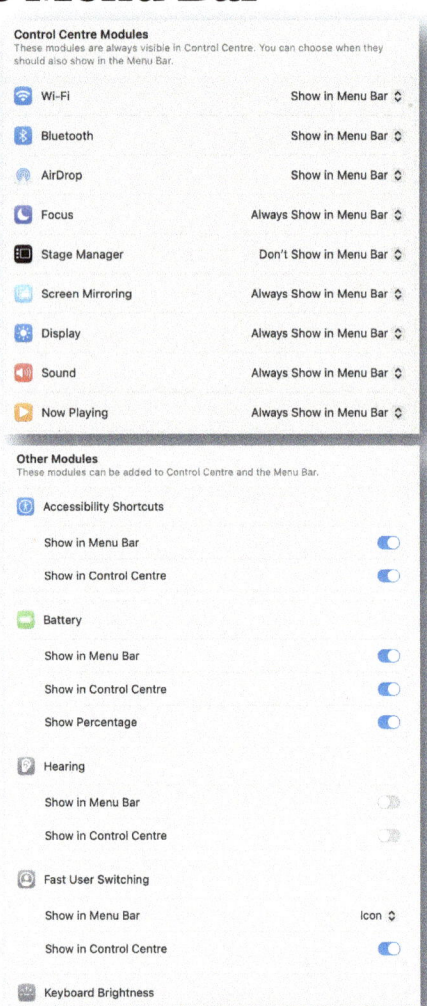

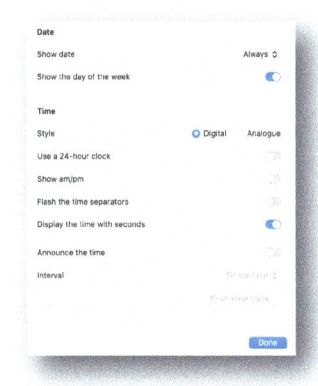

Menus and the Menu Bar

Using the Control Centre

Click the ⊟ icon to view the Control Centre (right).

When you hover your cursor over any of the controls shown in the Control Centre, a > symbol will appear on the right (as shown for Wi-Fi in image on right).

This indicates that there are some further options for the Control – so click the symbol to view these options.

For example, clicking on the > that appears when I hover over Wi-Fi provides me with the Wi-Fi options (image on right) – the same options that I get if I click on the Wi-Fi symbol that I also see in my Menu Bar.

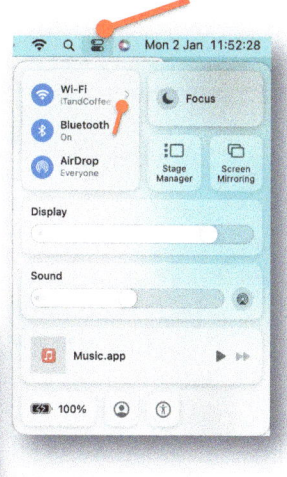

Even if the > doesn't appear, clicking on an icon in the Control Centre will show some options for that control – or allow you to adjust somethinge (e.g. turn up/down display brightnes or sound).

Spotlight Search 🔍

The right-hand side of the menu bar shows the **Spotlight Search** option (the magnifying glass).

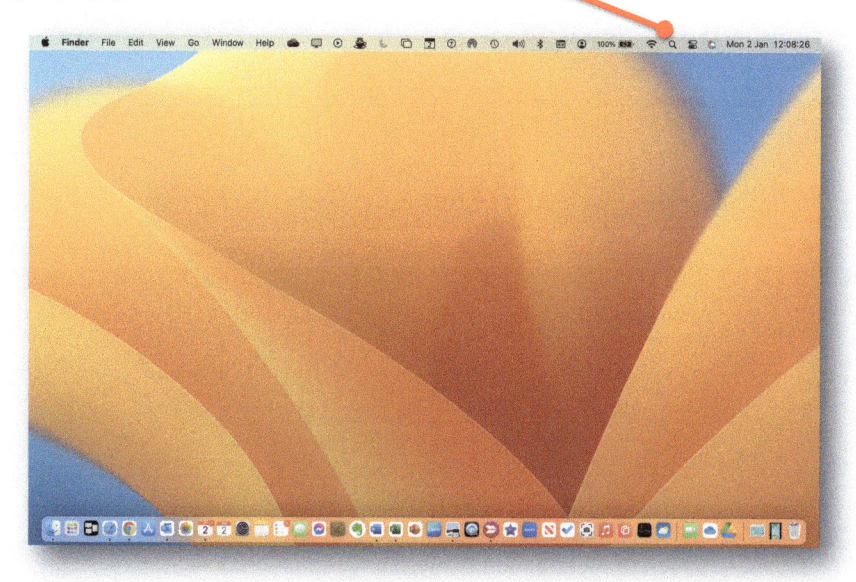

Menus and the Menu Bar

Spotlight Search allows the Mac to be searched for any file, folder, app, message, contact and more. A web search phrase can be typed here.

A mathematical calculation can be entered for a quick answer.

It is a great way of gaining quick access to anything on your Mac or on the Web.

I use it most frequently to open apps that don't show in my Dock.

Siri

macOS Sierra (2016) heralded the arrival of Siri on the Mac.

Mac's Siri can be activated by clicking the Siri symbol in the menu bar, at top right. As with your iPhone and iPad, just tell Siri what you need, or ask Siri a question.

Settings for Siri – including activating or de-activating 'Listen for "Hey Siri"' - can be found in **System Settings -> Siri & Spotlight**.

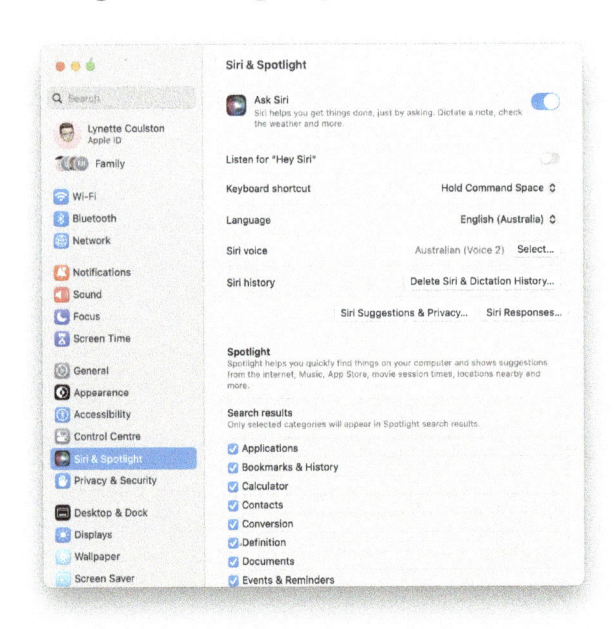

If you don't see the Siri symbol in your Menu Bar, check your Control Centre setting for Siri, found in the **Menu Bar Only** section (which is the last section) of the **System Settings -> Control Centre** option.

32

Menus and the Menu Bar

Notification Centre

Under previous versions of macOS, the **Notification Centre** was found by clicking the right-most symbol on the menu bar, ☰.

This changed with macOS Big Sur, when this symbol disappeared – and made it less obvious where the Notification Centre is found!

Since macOS Big Sur, the Notification Centre has been accessed by clicking on the time at top right of the Menu Bar.

Similar to the Notification Centre on the iPad and iPhone, the Mac's Notification Centre shows a summary of recent Notifications you may have missed (messages that pop up on your screen) PLUS snippets of information from various apps and features on my Mac – known as Widgets.

The set of widgets that appear in this area can be modified by scrolling to the bottom and choosing **Edit Widgets.**

We won't go into any great detail on the Widget topic in this guide – but the idea is that you choose a widget size (S, M, L) for any widget you wish to see in the Notification Centre and then then click the green + at top left to add it to the set of Widgets.

In the example on the right, I have chosen **Edit Widgets**, then clicked the **News** option in the left sidebar and then chosen the second (**Topic**) option and S (for small) widget size.

I click the + at top left of that widget preview to add it to my widget set (or drag it from the left to right side to add it),

33

Menus and the Menu Bar

then choose **Done** at bottom right to complete my Widget additions. While in that Edit mode, I can also choose the – (minus symbol) at top left of any already-added widget to remove it and drag my widgets around to re-organise them.

Visit -> **System Settings** -> **Notifications** to choose what apps are allowed to provide notifications, the form of the notification and whether the notification goes into the Notification Centre.

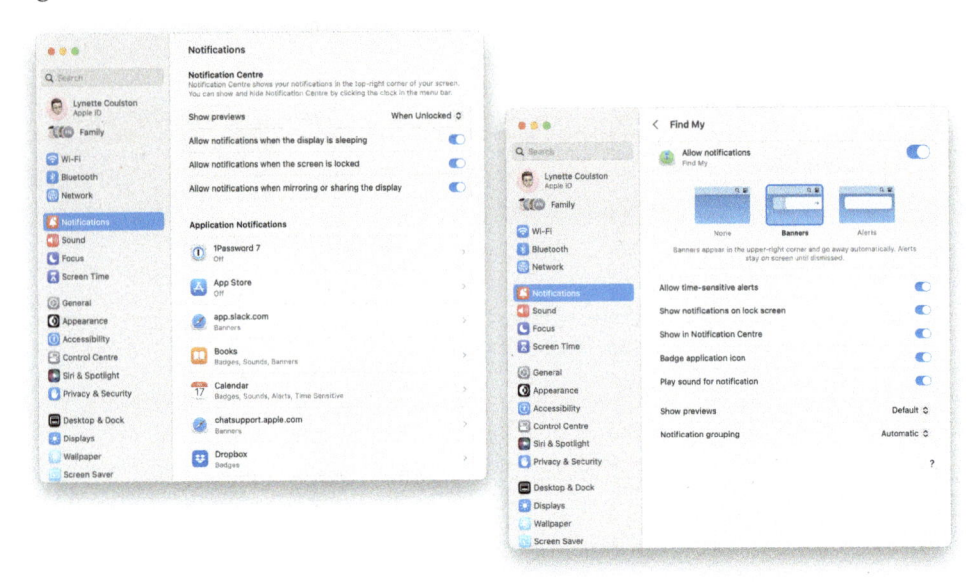

Click each app in the list under **Application Notifications** to choose to turn off app notifications that are not required or turn on notifications that are required.

As on the iPad and iPhone, you can choose the 'notification style' for each app –

- Alerts (which stay on screen until dismissed),
- Banners (which appear then disappear), or
- None (if that App should not provide notifications)

and whether notifications should appear on the Lock Screen, in the Notification Centre, whether they should provide a badge on the app's icon in the Dock, whether a sound should play, and whether previews of the notification content should (or shouldn't) appear when the Mac is locked.

The image above right shows an example of the app-specific Notification settings for the **Find My** app.

Connecting to Wi-Fi

Connecting to Wi-Fi on a Mac is easy. Look for the Wi-Fi symbol in the menu/status bar - it will look like one of the following:

Click on this symbol (which is over to the top right of the screen).

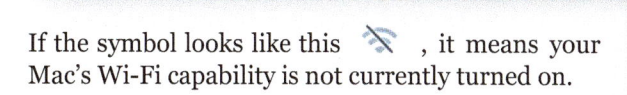

If the symbol looks like this , it means your Mac's Wi-Fi capability is not currently turned on.

Click on the symbol and then drag the circle across to the right (to give a blue background) to turn on the Wi-Fi capability of your Mac.

If Wi-Fi is on, your Mac will show a list of the nearby Wireless Networks that could be joined.

If it has 'remembered' any nearby Wi-Fi, then it will usually automatically join that network.

Those Wireless networks that your Mac has previously joined will be shown under the heading **Known Networks**.

Choose **Other Networks** to see any other nearby Wireless Networks.

Click on the name of the Wireless Network that you would like to join, then enter the password for that network, then **Join**.

If the password is correctly entered, you will be connected to that network and will appear on the left of the network name - to indicate that you are connected.

The Wi-Fi symbol in the status bar will change to

Once you have connected to a Wi-Fi network, your Mac will 'remember' that network and its password – so that it will automatically connect to the network whenever you are within its range.

35

Connecting to Wi-Fi

Connecting to a new Wi-Fi network does not impact any other Wi-Fi networks to which you have previously connected.

Your Mac will remember them all, and automatically connect whenever a known network is in range. (That is, unless you have specifically chosen not to Auto-join that Network. We won't cover this option as part of this introductory guide.)

Note that if the Wi-Fi symbol is greyed (instead of solid black), it means that your Mac's Wi-Fi is turned on, but there is no Wi-Fi network in range that it can connect to – so you will not have any internet.

The settings associated with Wi-Fi can be found in **System Settings -> Wi-Fi**.

In particular, click ⋯ the on the right of any **Known Networks** name to see options for that network.

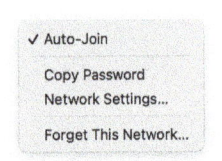

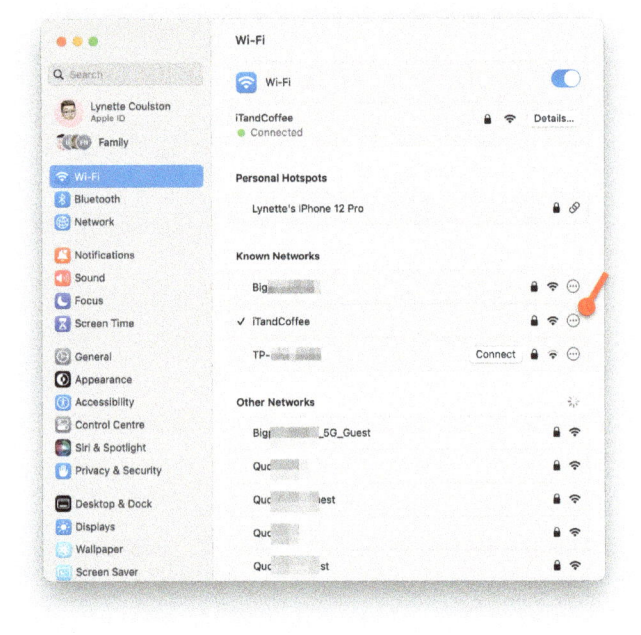

If you don't wish to automatically join a particular known network when it is nearby, untick the **Auto-Join** option.

There is the option to copy the network's **Password**, and to **Forget this Network** (which is sometimes necessary when your Mac has 'remembered' an old password that no longer seems to work).

The App Store on your Mac

Discovering the App Store

Just like for your iPad and iPhone, Apple has provided an App Store for the purchasing of Apps for your Mac.

The App Store icon can normally be found in the Dock (unless it has been removed). We'll look later at how to put an app back into the Dock if it has disappeared.

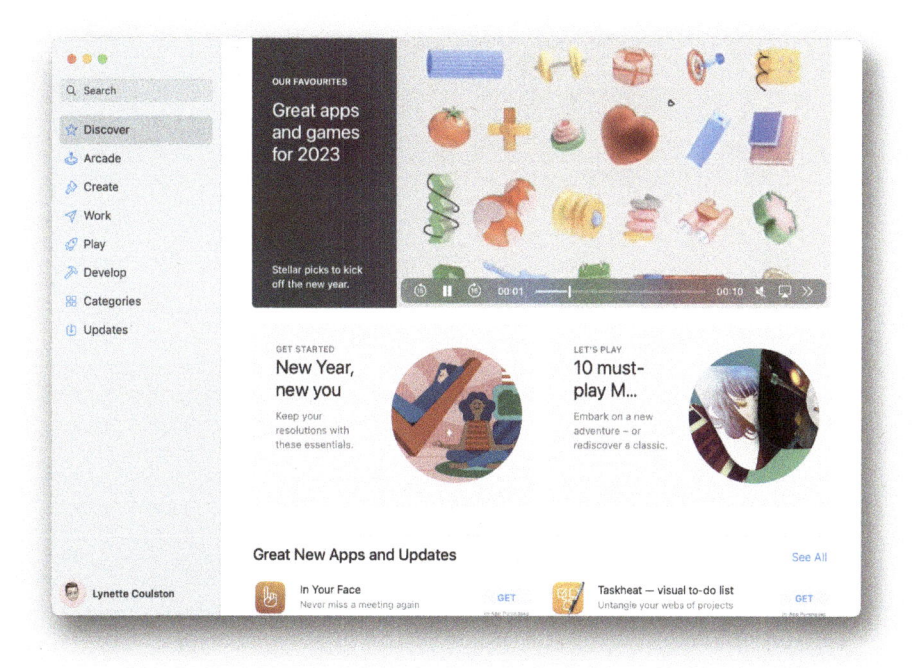

Different App Stores for Mac and iOS

Mac Apps are different to iPad/iPhone Apps – **an app purchased on an iPhone or iPad is not automatically available on the Mac**. In nearly all cases, the Mac version must be purchased (or downloaded) separately.

(Note. Those who purchase a new Mac with the M1 or M2 chip WILL be able to run iOS/iPad OS apps on their Mac. But, given this is only available for some Macs and is something for more advanced users, we won't cover this as part of this guide.)

The App Store on the Mac looks very similar to the App Store on your iOS device, and it is able to use the same iTunes account that is used on your iPad and iPhone. Any credit stored against that iTunes account can be used for Mac apps.

The App Store on your Mac

Any app purchased/downloaded on one Mac then can be used on any other Mac belonging to that person (or other family members – using iCloud's Family Sharing).

The App Store is also where any updates to your Mac's apps can be found, downloaded and installed.

Checking for App Updates

In macOS Mojave (2018), the App Store underwent significant changes to its design. The main options of the App Store now appear down the side (instead of along the top).

Click on the **Updates** option at the bottom of the sidebar list to see any updates that are yet to be applied to your Mac's apps.

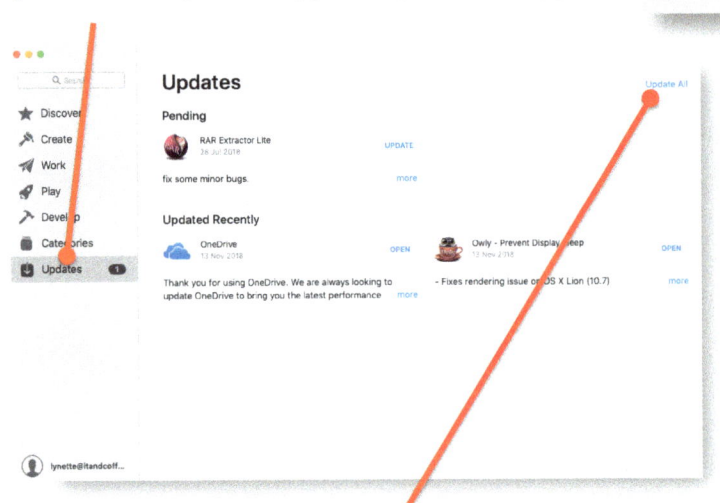

Choose to update individual apps, or Update All (top right) to apply all of the updates shown.

Have an 'explore' of the App store to see the sorts of apps you can get for Mac.

You will notice as you scroll down the Discover view that there are lots of free apps, as well as lots of useful 'paid' apps.

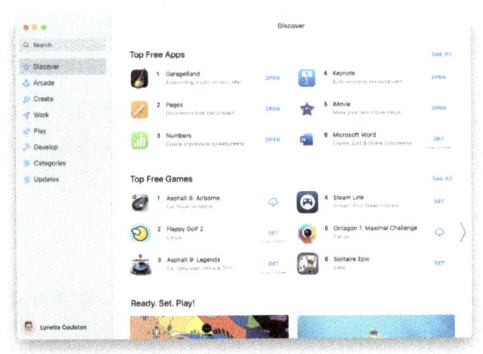

38

The App Store on your Mac

Automatic updates to your Apps

Rather than having to go and check for app updates on a regular basis, is it easier to set your Mac to do this automatically.

This can be set up from the Settings associated with your App Store app. Click the App Store menu at top left (it will be on right of the when the App Store app is currently active) and choose **Settings**.

Make sure the **Automatic Updates** option is ticked.

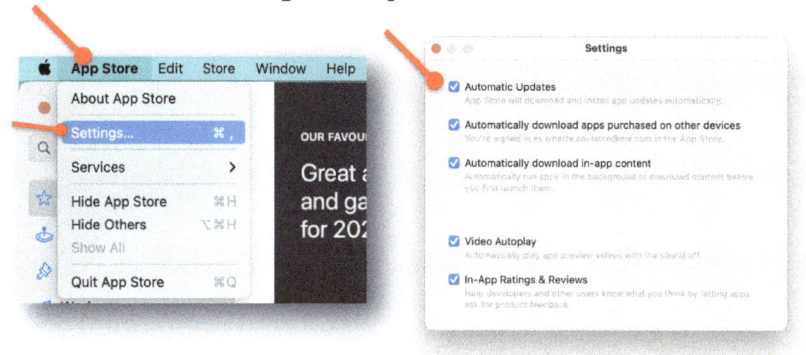

Getting Apps that are not in the App Store

It is best to try to only download apps that are in App Store, as these apps have been vetted by Apple as safe.

However, there are sometimes apps that are not available in the App Store.

One in particular that I have downloaded is **Dropbox**, which I downloaded from **Dropbox.com.** Another is **TeamViewer** from **Teamviewer.com.** In more recent years, many people have downloaded the **Zoom** app from the **Zoom.us** website.

If you do need to download an app that is not in the App Store, it may be necessary to first lower a security setting on your Mac. And, if you get a message like that shown above right, only choose **Open** if you are really confident that the app is authentic.

If the app that you have attempted to download is being blocked (ie Apple does not deem it to be from an identified developer), you will temporarily need to lower your

The App Store on your Mac

security. Once again, make sure that you are absolutely sure that the app (and the site that you download it from) is safe.

Your security settings for apps can be found in **System Settings -> Privacy & Security**. Scroll down to the section headed **Security**.

You will see two options under the heading **Allow apps downloaded from**. I leave this set to **App Store and identified developers**.

When you try to change this setting, you will be asked to provide your Mac's administrator password.

However, there are times when you may find that you need to download and run something that is blocked due to this setting.

If the App is from an unidentified developer, you will see a message advising that opening of the app has been blocked – something like that shown here.

You can still open the App – as long as you are sure it is safe. To do this, go to the **Applications** folder in Finder (where the app has been installed)

In Finder, right-click (or two-finger click, if applicable) the app, choose Open from the menu, and in the window that appears, click **Open**.

Enter your Mac's administrator name and password when prompted, and the app should then run.

That app is then set as a permanent exception to the security rules, and will open without any issue in future.

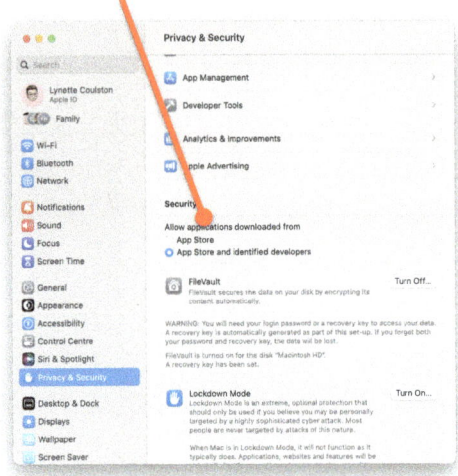

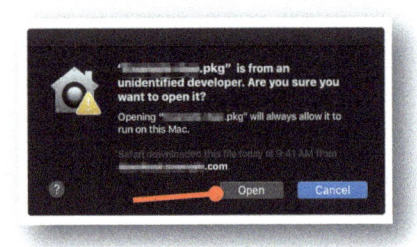

40

Mission Control

Viewing all the windows that are open

When there are lots of windows open on your Mac, it can be difficult to find the App window that you are looking for.

Since Big Sur

Mission Control is Apple's solution to this problem – and it has a revamped icon that arrived with Big Sur in 2020 (see image top right).

Mission Control gives a 'bird's-eye view' of all the open windows and apps.

Pre-Big Sur

It usually appears in the Dock. On many Macs, it can be accessed from some Apple Keyboards by pressing the **F3** key.

It can also be accessed by pressing the keyboard shortcut **Control-⬆**.

If you have a MacBook with trackpad, try swiping up with three or four fingers on this trackpad. On a mouse, you may be able to double-tap with two fingers to activate Mission Control.

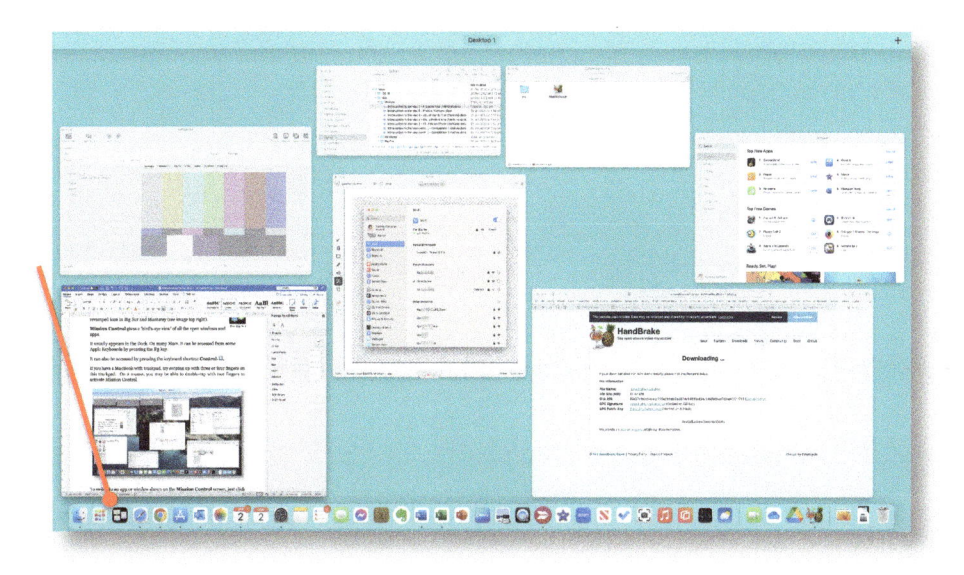

To switch to an app or window shown on the **Mission Control** screen, just click on it.

Exit **Mission Control** (if you don't want to click a window) by pressing its App icon in the dock, **F3** (if available), **Control-⬆** or the **esc** key at top left on the keyboard. If you swiped up with three/four fingers, swipe back down with the same three fingers to exit **Mission Control**. On the mouse, double-tap two fingers again to exit.

Mission Control

If Mission Control is missing from the Dock

In the next section we will talk about something called Launchpad, which shows all the apps on the Mac. If your Mission Control icon is missing from the Dock, you will be able to drag it back there from Launchpad.

Setting up your Mission Control preferences

You will find your settings for Mission Control in **System Settings**. Previously, there was a separate option for Mission Control. These settings are now in the **Mission Control** section at the end of the **Desktop & Dock** settings.

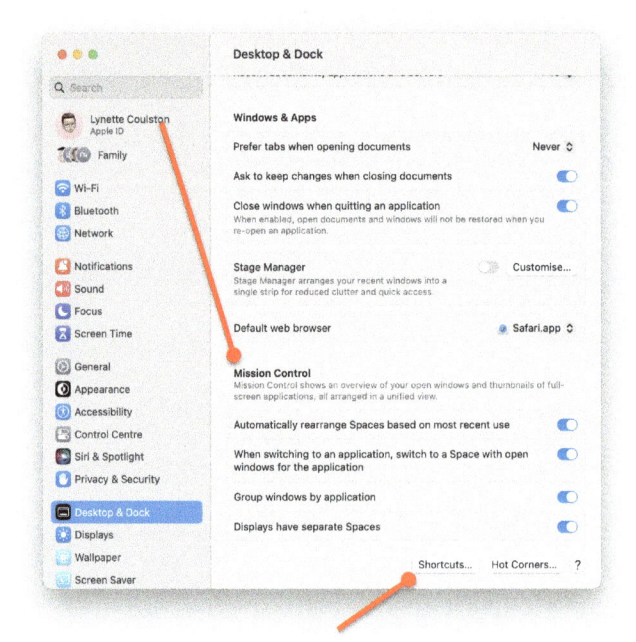

In particular, from here you can change the keyboard shortcut that is used to activate this feature.

Click the **Shortcuts** button at the very bottom.

You will see you can also define the shortcuts for **Application Windows**, **Show Desktop**, and **Show Dashboard**.

Mission Control

The other place where you can adjust the settings for activating Mission Control (and another feature called App Exposé – covered next) is from the **Mouse** and **Trackpad** settings of **System Settings** - from the **More Gestures** section.

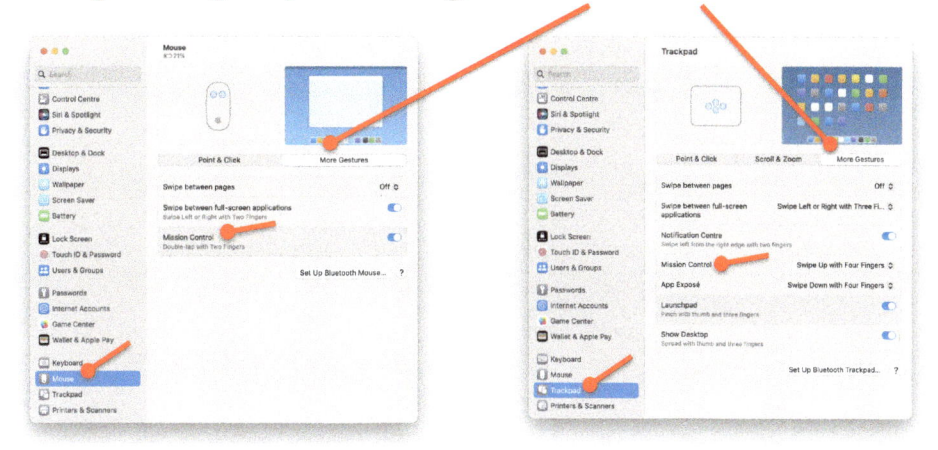

You can turn on or off the mouse/trackpad gesture for activating features, and (in some cases) modify the gesture that is used – for example, choose between 3 or 4 fingers on the Trackpad.

App Exposé

If you are like me, you can often end up with multiple windows open for the same App. Apple provides a quick way of seeing and switching between the open windows for the same app – using a feature called **App Exposé**, which is part of Mission Control

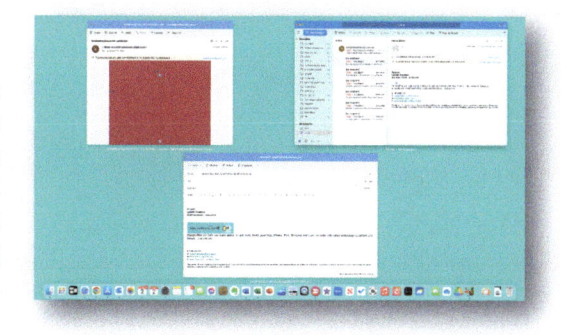

App Exposé can be activated using

- Control ▼ (keyboard shortcut)
- Swipe down on trackpad with 3 or 4 fingers (choose this in System Settings – see App Exposé option, shown in the image at top right, below the Mission Control option).

Just click on the window you wish to activate to make it the current window (and exit App Exposé mode).

To exit this mode without choosing a window, simply press the Esc key, or Control ▼ again. If you are using the trackpad of a MacBook, you can also swipe up with 3 or 4 fingers (depending on your preference) to close App Exposé.

Launchpad

We have looked at The Dock for showing all your favourite and frequently used Apps.

But where do you find all the OTHER Apps that are on your Mac.

Launchpad is like the iPhone Home Screen

All Apps on your Mac can be seen using your Launchpad app which should appear in your Dock.

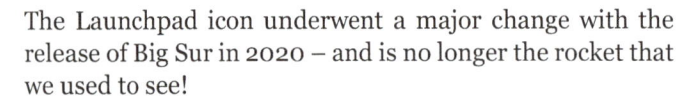

The Launchpad icon underwent a major change with the release of Big Sur in 2020 – and is no longer the rocket that we used to see!

Since Big Sur   Pre-Big Sur

Launchpad will provide a set of screens (1 or more) that are like the Home Screens on your iPad and iPhone.

Swipe between the screens (single finger swipe across the mouse or two-finger swipe across the trackpad) to see more apps - or click on the dots below the apps to move between the screens of apps.

Click once on the required App to open it.

If you can't see the required App, use the search field that is at the top of the Launchpad screen to search for the app you seek.

44

Launchpad

Put Apps into an App Group

Just like on the iPad and iPhone, Apps can be dragged on top of each other to form an **App Group** – and given whatever name you like.

The **Other** group will already appear in Launchpad, containing a range of Utility apps – some of which we will feature as part of this series of **Introduction to the Mac** guides.

Drag 'Favourite' apps from Launchpad to the Dock

If you see an App in **Launchpad** that you would like to have appear in the **Dock** permanently, just drag it from Launchpad down onto the **Dock**, into the desired position.

The apps will move aside to make room for the new arrival.

Alternatively, while the App is running, **right click** its icon in the Dock, choose **Options** and click **Keep in Dock** (so that it is ticked – as shown below).

The App will still be visible in **Launchpad**, even if you drag it to the Dock or choose to **Keep in Dock** using the method described above.

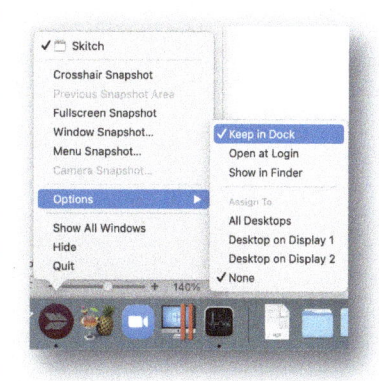

As mentioned earlier, the Dock is simply providing a shortcut for accessing your favourite apps.

Other ways of opening LaunchPad

On Mac keyboards that have a physical row of Function keys along the top, pressing the F4 key will show the Launchpad.

If you have a trackpad, pinching inwards with your thumb and four fingers will show Launchpad.

If you have a MacBook with a Touch Bar (aka Control Bar), you will find the Launchpad on that bar.

You may need to expand the bar first to be able to see the controls shown in the image above, but touching the arrow indicated here.

Launchpad

Adding Launchpad back to the Dock

If Launchpad is no longer appearing in your Dock, it can be easily added back again.

I find the easiest way to do this is to use Spotlight Search to search for the Launchpad app. When I do this, Launchpad's app appears as the first result and includes the icon on left.

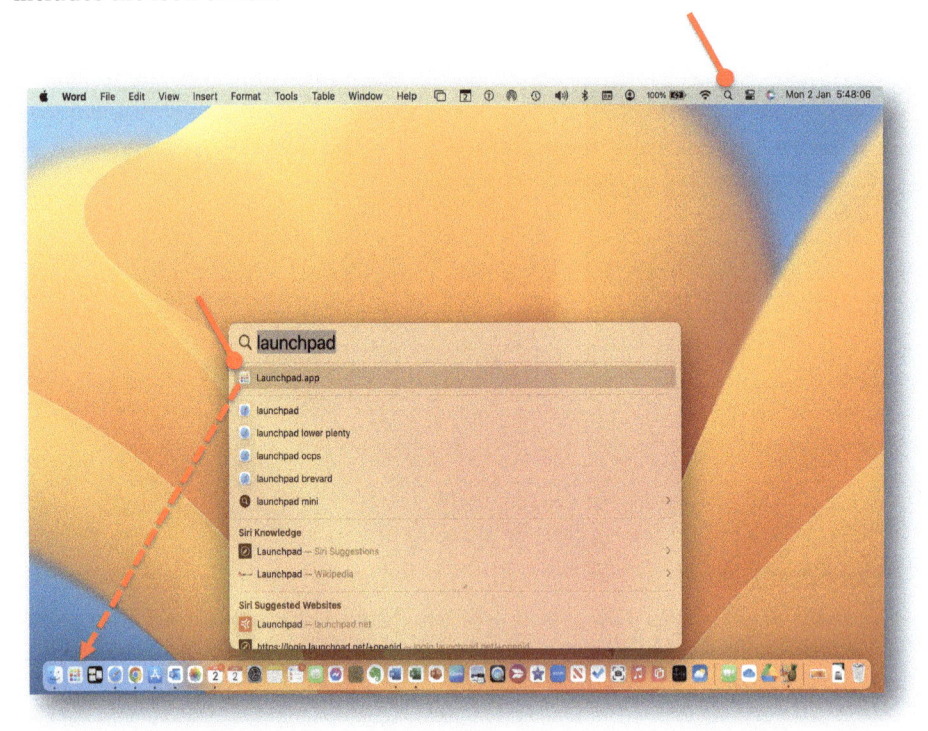

I can then drag that first search result item down onto the Dock, into the required position.

Launchpad will then remain as an icon in the Dock.

This technique for adding apps to the Dock works for any other App that is not currently a permanent feature of the Dock.

Stage Manager

A new look for Desktop in macOS Ventura – Stage Manager

macOS Ventura has brought a new way of organising all the app Windows that are open on our Macs. It is a feature that can be optionally enabled from **System Settings** and is called **Stage Manager**.

If you have used the Mac for a while, you may be familiar with the 'mess' that you may see on your screen when you have several apps and windows open at once.

For example, as I write this page of this guide, here is what my screen looks like, with all the windows open behind it.

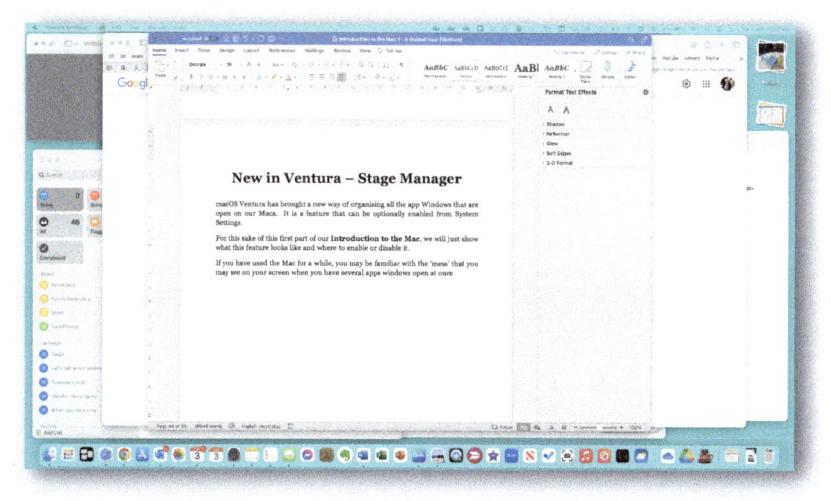

If I turn on **Stage Manager**, my screen looks so much tidier!

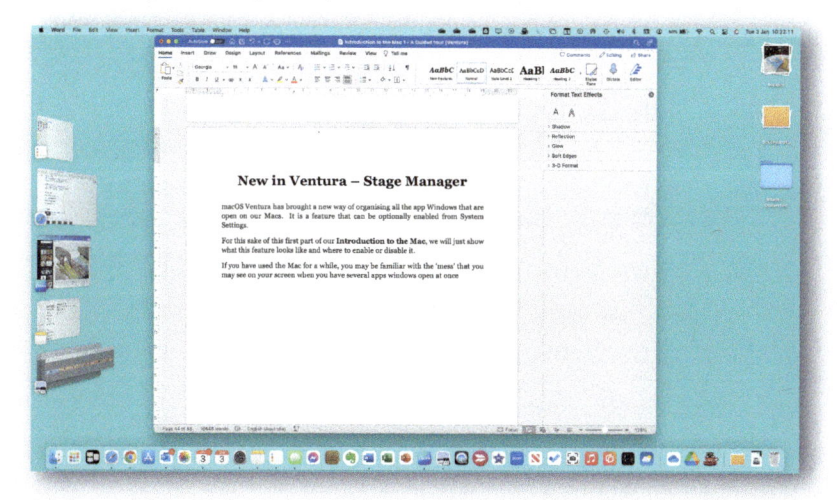

Stage Manager

Stage Manager is designed to help you keep your screen more organised when you are working with multiple apps and app windows at once, but want to focus mainly on one app at a time. The non-active apps and their windows appear on the left side of the screen, and only the currently active app has 'centre stage' (and can be moved around).

You can click any of the app thumbnails on the left side to make that app active – and the previously active app will become a thumbnail on the left.

Depending on your settings, you can choose to show all of the windows for a selected app at once or show them one at a time (clicking the thumbnail on left to go to each window).

Stage Manager can be activated (or deactivated) from **System Settings -> Desktop & Dock**. It is found about two-thirds of the way down the set of options.

Choose the **Customise** button to see the set of options available for Stage Manager. You will see that you can choose to show Desktop items at all times (for those files and folders you store on the Desktop and make your choice about whether clicking on the left thumbnails brings up all Windows for the app, or just one at a time.

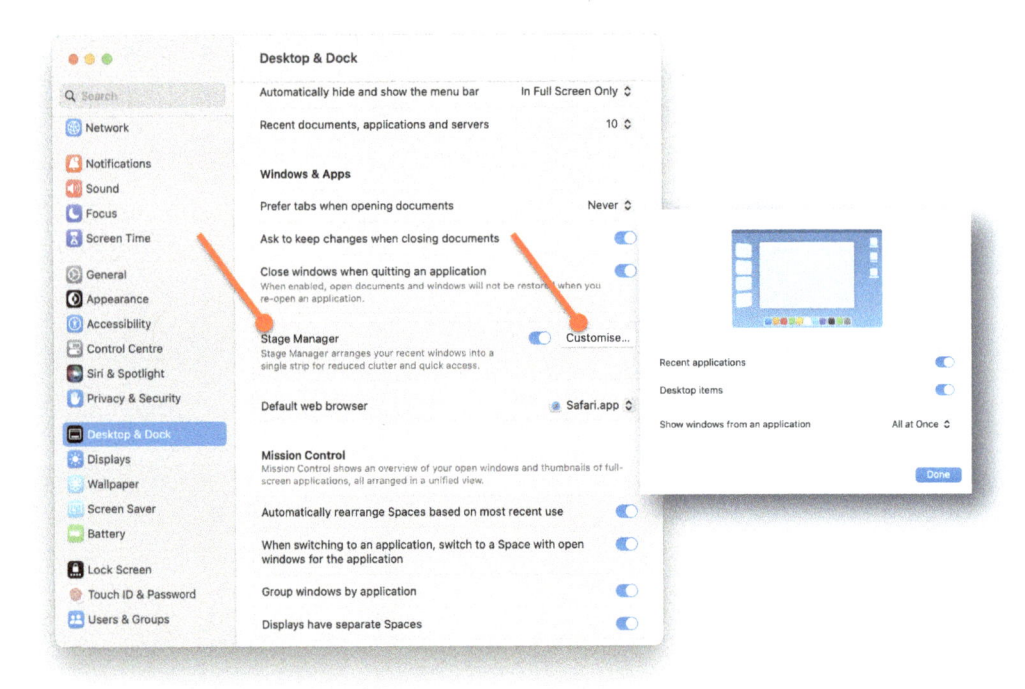

It is worth checking out this new feature. I must say that I do like it – sometimes! I have been turning it on and off depending on what I am working on.

The Bin (or Trash Can)

The right-most icon in the Mac's Dock is the Bin (or Trash Can).

The Bin is where all files and folders go when you delete them.

Files and folders can be placed in the Bin by

- dragging them on top of the Bin icon,
- by 'right-clicking' on the File/Folder and choosing **Move to Bin**
- by using the keyboard shortcut **Command-delete**.

It is important to note that the Bin *only contains files and folders*.

Deleted **Mail** messages appear in the **Deleted** mailbox of the Mail App.

Deleted **Photos** appear in the **Recently Deleted** album of the **Photos** app (if deleted from within that app).

Deleted **Notes** appear in the **Recently Deleted** folder of the Notes app.

It is important to regularly empty your Bin – to free up storage that is still being used by the deleted files. This storage is only freed up after you have emptied the Bin.

To see the contents of the Bin, click on the symbol in the Dock. You will see that the Bin looks like any Finder folder (which we look at in more detail in the **Files, Folders and Finder** guide.)

To Empty the bin, choose **Empty** at top right.

Or right-click on the Bin icon in the Dock and choose **Empty Bin**.

If there is a file or folder in the Bin that you wish to put back (i.e. you didn't mean to delete it), right-click on it and choose **Put Back**.

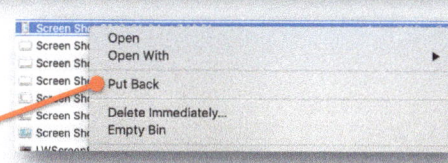

Some Common Keyboard Shortcuts

Keyboard Shortcuts are combinations of keys that will perform some function that would otherwise require the selection of a menu option, and which can really speed up certain activities on your Mac.

There is a huge number of Keyboard shortcuts, more than any of us can remember - so I won't try to list them all here. Instead, here is a list of those that I find myself using on a regular basis.

It may be worth bookmarking this set of pages, so that you can easily refer to them in future.

Managing Windows, Dock, Apps

Shortcut	Description
Command-Shift-D	Hide or Unhide Dock
Command-M	Minimise the current window
Command-H	Hide all Windows of the current App
Command-Option-H	Hide all Windows of apps other than the current App
Command-Q	Quit the currently active app.
Command-Option-Esc	Open the Force Quit screen to force quit an app.
Command-Comma (,)	Open Preferences for the front app.
Command-P	Print
Command-S	Save
Space bar	**Quick Look** at the selected item in Finder
Command-Space Bar	Show or hide **Spotlight Search**
Command-Tab	Switch apps
Command-N	Open a new document or window.

Some Common Keyboard Shortcuts

Cut, Copy, Paste, Select, Undo

Shortcut	Description
Command-X	Cut: Remove the selected item/text and copy it to the Clipboard (an area of memory on the Mac). *(Doesn't apply in Finder)*
Command-C	Copy the selected item or text to the Clipboard.
Command-V	Paste the contents of the Clipboard into the current position. For Finder, Command-V performs a copy of the selected file/folder. (To move instead of copy, use Command-Option-V) In text editing, Command V pastes whatever is in the Clipboard (an area of the Mac's memory where copied content is saved, waiting to be 'pasted')
Command-Z	Undo the previous action.
Command-Shift-Z	Redo what you just undid.
Command-A	Select All items.

Sleep, log out, and shut down shortcuts

Shortcut	Description
Power button	Tap to turn on your Mac or wake your Mac from sleep.
	Hold for 1.5 seconds while your Mac is awake to display a dialog asking if you want to restart, sleep, or shut down.
	Hold for 5 seconds to force your Mac to turn off.
Command–Control–Power button	Quit all apps, then restart your Mac. If any open documents have unsaved changes, you'll be asked whether you want to save them.
Command–Option–Control–Power button	Quit all apps, then shut down your Mac. If any open documents have unsaved changes, you'll be asked whether you want to save them.

Some Common Keyboard Shortcuts

Document/typing shortcuts

Note. Some of these shortcuts are not applicable in Microsoft apps, where Control has different functions.

Shortcut	Description
Command-B	Bold selected text
Command-I	Italics format for selected text
Command-U	Underline selected text
Control-D or fn-Delete	Delete the character on the right (for keyboards that only have a 'backspace' key)
Option-Delete	Delete the word on the left
Control-K	Delete from current position to end of sentence or paragraph.
Fn–Up Arrow	Scroll one page upwards
Fn–Down Arrow	Scroll one page downwards
Fn–Left Arrow	Jump to the beginning of the document/text
Fn–Right Arrow	Jump to the end of the document/text
Command–Up Arrow	Move the cursor position to the beginning of the document.
Command–Down Arrow	Move the cursor position to the end of the document.
Command–Left Arrow	Move cursor position to the start of the current line.
Command–Right Arrow	Move the cursor position to the end of the current line.
Control-A	Move to the beginning of the line or paragraph. (Not applicable in Microsoft products.)
Control-E	Move to the end of a line or paragraph. (Not applicable in Microsoft products.)
Command-Option-C	Copy Style: Copy the formatting settings of the selected item to the Clipboard.
Command-Option-V	Paste Style: Apply the copied style to the selected item.
Command-Shift-Option-V	Paste and Match Style: Apply the style of the surrounding content to the item pasted within that content.

Other Books in this Series

Files, Folders & Finder

Backups, Apps & Preferences

All Sorts of Handy Tips

The Photos App

Videos about the Mac

Learn even more about your Mac with a range of Videos about the Mac, available on the iTandCoffee website.

For more information about iTandCoffee class videos and user guides, visit

www.itandcoffee.com.au/videos

www.itandcoffee.com.au/guides

Ingram Content Group UK Ltd.
Milton Keynes UK
UKHW050729190723
425403UK00010B/79